ROY

"THAT'S HOW HE SEES ME"

BY RENEE MINOR JOHNSON

However, you are chosen people, a royal priesthood, a holy nation, people who belong to God. You were chosen to tell about the excellent qualities of God, who called you out of darkness into his marvelous light.

1 Peter 2:9 (GW)

ChampionsWithin Kingdom Builders
ISBN-13: 978-0692931769

Published By: Terry "Ranger" Johnson, Sr.
ChampionsWithin Kingdom Builders
E-mail: championswithin2@yahoo.com
Website: www.rangerjohnson.com

Editor: Regina Bryant McKenzie,
Educator GPISD

Front Cover Photo: Haylie Noel Photography,
haylienoelphotography@gmail.com

Back Cover Photo: Alanie Sayer,
alaniesayerphoto@gmail.com

Book Formatting: Ramona Latham,
rslatham@bellsouth.net

Printed in the USA

CONTENTS

DEDICATION

I would like to dedicate this book to my parents, the Late Pastor Willie Minor Jr. and Orleana S. Minor. If they were alive today they would tell everyone they met that I had published my second book (especially my dad). I have two amazing big sisters, and they would agree with me in saying that our daddy made us feel like we could succeed in anything that we put our hands to. Dad is no longer with us; however, my sisters and I often encourage each other by repeating one of his phrases... "yes, yes, yes... you can do it girls, you can do it."

Daddy was one of the greatest cheerleaders ever!! He would encourage anybody, anytime, anywhere. He always spoke affirming words over our family. He believed in tapping into the greatness inside of people. He was a true visionary. His vision for our family and his community was far beyond our understanding.

If you were a singer, he would say " yes, yes, yes...... 'You should try to get your songs on the radio".... If you had the ability to recite a poem or poetry without fear, or stumbling over your words, he would say..." yes, yes, yes... You would be a great lawyer; you should go to law school".

I've learned in my journey that words are seeds and whatever word/seeds you plant, will grow. I guess that would mean that daddy was a cheerleader and a farmer (smile). Daddy was known to plant seeds of encouragement everywhere he went and with whomever he met.

Back in 2002, when my husband and I developed Champions Within, daddy started planting more seeds. He began to say... "yes, yes, yes... when are you going to write your book?" Of course, that was the farthest thing from my mind. My dad and my husband were cut from the same cloth and they often spoke the same language. My husband was totally onboard with the whole book writing thing. He published two books before I even believed I could write one book. It took me a long time to trust that I had anything within me worth writing about. Clearly, I was lacking in confidence. I had to reach into God's word and allow Philippians 1:6 to take root.... I had to become confidently sure that God, who began a good work within me, would keep helping me grow in his grace until his task within me is complete.

As I ubered through life believing in others, and cheering for others to succeed, I failed to reflect on the cheers from the cheerleaders God had assigned to me. Finally, in 2012 we published my first book "A Game Called Life"; It was a children's book. It wasn't too long after my first book was published that my "cheerleading daddy" began to ask... (in his James Earl Jones voice) ... "Yes, yes, yes... when are you going to get started on your next book?" Well, in my mind's eye, it took me 10 years to produce a small children's book (so I guess 2022 would be the answer to that question).

It must have been somewhere along that time, that his cheering and seed planting begin to take root. Here it is, 2017, and I'm on book number two. Words really are seeds and the seeds you plant will grow. I guess I'll make a very important point here, it is always necessary for us to be careful with our words... they have power. Whatever you say... you will see.

I'm more than grateful that we had a father that inspired and encouraged us to be the best we could be and to always give our best effort in whatever we put our hands to. Even when I didn't make the best decisions in life, his vision for my life never changed. One of his favorite scriptures was Proverbs 3:5-6; He truly lived by it. Our father made a constant effort to trust God, and speak what he believed to see in us. This reminds me of the scripture in Psalms 27:13 when David said...

"I believe that I will see the goodness of the LORD in this world of the living."

I am grateful for the parents that God gave us and for the foundation that was laid for my sisters and I. Dad and Mom have gone to be with the Lord, and I know that they are amongst the great cloud of witnesses continuously cheering us on. Thanks Dad and Mom for teaching us how to trust God and run the race!!!

Therefore, since we are surrounded by such a great cloud of witnesses, let us throw off everything that hinders and the sin that so

easily entangles. And let us run with perseverance the race marked out for us,
Hebrews 12:1 (NIV)

Trust in the LORD with all your heart; do not depend on your own understanding. ⁶Seek his will in all you do, and he will show you which path to take.
Proverbs 3:5-6 (NLT)

So, do not throw away this confident trust in the Lord. Remember the great reward it brings you!
Hebrews 10:35 (NLT)

being confident of this very thing, that he who began a good work in you will complete it until the day of Jesus Christ.
Philippians 1:6 (WEB)

FOREWORD

"Royalty...That's How He Sees Me"

Often times in our lives we do not see ourselves truly as we should. In this generation alone, many of us lack really knowing who we are and this can lead to a crisis of identity. Oxford American Dictionary defines *"Identity"* in a general context as the fact of being who or what a person or thing is. So, the question is who determines that fact? Also, the above-mentioned dictionary defines *"identity crisis"*, (within a psychological context) as a period of uncertainty and confusion in which a person's **sense of identity becomes insecure**, typically due to a change in their expected aims or role in society. This definition invokes inquiry of who determines or influences the expectation of who we are?

As for myself, I suffered an identity crisis for many years. I was unaware of my insecurities; I was always wondering who I was, why I was here, and what was my purpose . I used to think that I was as others perceived me to be. I believe unconsciously, I felt as though my job (or career of choice at the time) gave an accurate description of who I was. This was a lengthy cycle. During my on-going journey of spiritual self-discovery, I came across a Scripture that opened my eyes, and I begin to see and feel differently about myself. Romans 8:38-39 gave me a personal revelation of God's love for me (in a fatherly way).

38 For I am persuaded, that neither death, nor life, nor angels, nor principalities, nor powers, nor things present, nor things to come,39 Nor height, nor depth, nor any other creature, shall be able to separate us from the love of God, which is in Christ Jesus our Lord.
Romans 8:38-39 (KJV)

I believe that this book, written by Renee Johnson, (my dear sister in Christ and long-time friend) will help you begin to take a fresh journey to understanding the greatness, beauty, and significance waiting to be discovered within every reader! I believe one Word from the Lord can change the way we see and respond to our daily circumstances and situations.

The *"Royalty Declaration"* that she included at the beginning of this book will help you change your vocabulary and encourage you to articulate who you are through the eyes of God. We can be assured that what He says about all of us is pure, true, and is filled with His grace, love, and affection.

As you explore each chapter, you will see that Renee uses the Word of God, personal experiences, and her unique sense of nurturing, to exhort, encourage, and implore you to Rise-up.

Over the years as her sister-friend, she has helped me to become more nurturing and compassionate towards others; as my nature is to encourage, but with a stronger hand. As I observed her approach of gentleness and consideration of other people, her style of engagement still inspires me today. It reminds me that daily, we have an opportunity to choose to love others like Jesus. My prayer is that you embrace the words written in this book and know that God has compelled her, for such a time as this, to share her version of His love towards us. Embrace the precious gift of our true identity. It is available to all of us through His Only Son, Jesus Christ. I am confident that you will be able to find the rich and practical nuggets she leaves on every line within each chapter.

Bridgett Barnes
Bridgett Barnes Ministries,
Bakersfield, CA.

ROYALTY DECLARATION

This royalty declaration was designed for you. Allow the seed of these words to be planted in your heart and as one plants and one waters, God shall bring the increase.

It is my heart's desire to use every gift I possess, in every area of influence I have, to encourage and inspire you to live the abundant life God intended. I want the life that I live and the words that I speak to stir up a hunger for purpose within you. I hope to provoke you to fight for your dreams…. fight for your destiny. In doing so, you must remember that you cannot allow the issues of life, past hurts, current situations, or circumstances to distract you while in pursuit of your divine purpose. You must not give an ear to the "naysayer's".

Naysayers are individuals who deny, oppose, or are skeptical about something you are called to do. Naysayers can steal your dreams and kill your self-esteem.

In John 10:10, Jesus says, "The thief only comes in order to steal, kill, and destroy. I have come in order that you might have life— life in all its fullness". The enemy wants to kill your dreams, steal your self-esteem, and disrupt your path to your destiny. Our Heavenly Father has other plans... plans to prosper us and give us hope and a future (Jeremiah 29:11). His prosperous plans are made available to us through Christ Jesus.

From this day forward commit to connect with those who are dream builders and with those who help stir up a hunger for greatness within you. Pursue excellence in all that you do. This spirit of excellence goes far beyond the four walls of the church; it includes giving your best effort in all that you do in your day-to-day endeavors (at home, in your school work, and on your job). The bible tells us in Colossians 3:23 to do all that we do as unto the Lord. Be open and willing to allow your life to be a vessel that God's spirit can flow through... a conduit. Let a royal spirit of excellence become your lifestyle, your attitude. This attribute is the pathway to your destiny. Job 22:28 says..."Thou shalt also decree a thing, and it shall be established unto thee: and the light shall shine upon thy ways". So, begin each day decreeing and declaring the word of God over your life.

Start each day renewing your mind with the word of God (this leads to a transformation). Make a declaration to yourself that you are God's creation and start living like you believe every word He says about you. You are not what you've done or where you're from... You are not who people say you are. You are who God says you are...**Fearfully and Wonderfully Made... more than a Conqueror**, an **Overcomer, Crowned with Glory**. You were created with a purpose for a purpose. I decree and declare that you shall begin to see yourself through the Father's eyes...He sees you as **ROYALTY!!**

I AM A QUEEN

By Renee Johnson

I am a Queen
My beauty is fearfully and wonderfully made.
I was created with a purpose, for a purpose...
a purpose that I shall fulfill.

I have gifts and talents designed only for me.
And I will use them to make a difference in the
world from sea to shiny sea...

I have no need to imitate anyone,
I'm an original.
From the top of my head to the soles of my feet;
from the inside out, I am whole and complete;

I walk with my head held high, in a spirit of
dignity,
wearing a crown, be-jeweled with wisdom,
knowledge, and integrity.
I never lower my standards for anyone.
I am Royalty...
I am a Queen....

Though I have experienced misfortunes and mishaps in my life,

And I may have been knocked down a time or two,

But staying down is what I **REFUSE** to do!

I'm not ashamed of where I'm from

I've turn from the wrong that I've done

Embracing the new creature, I have become...

I am no longer imprisoned or entrapped by my past.

I choose to forget those things that are behind me

And press toward the mark of the prize ahead of me

The prize of a future filled with hope, and, prosperity.

I'm not a carbon copy of a great original

I am an original...

I AM A QUEEN!!

Can you relate to a section of the poem?

_____

_____

_____

If so, which section and why?

_____

_____

_____

Have you allowed naysayers/situations to discourage you in your pursuit of your purpose?

_____

_____

_____

Have you allowed your self-perception to hinder you in pursuing your dreams?

_____

_____

_____

CHAPTER 1

MANUFACTURER'S MANUAL

The manufacturer's manual is the instructional guide that is usually found in the front of purchased products. This guide consists of the basic operational instructions to be followed in order to receive the full, maximum performance and to avoid unnecessary damages to the said product. However, if there are any major malfunctions, it is suggested to consult the manufacturer's Manual. Why? Because the maker of the product knows more about the product than the proposed user.

The manufacturer gives the product a name and the purpose for use. In most owners' manuals, it states that in order to stay in line with the warranty, all repairs must be done by the manufacturer of the product. If the owner decides not to follow the suggested guidelines noted in the manufacture's manual, it cancels out the benefits that go along with the warranty package. Now allow me to use this physical example to open your spiritual eyes….. Many times, we wonder why we are not reaping the full benefits that come with our royal position as sons and daughters of the "Most High". Well, when we choose not to follow the suggested recommendations located in the manual, we forfeit our full benefits.

When we are broken spiritually, feeling disconnected, and needing restoration we should always go back to the one who created us... "OUR MAKER". The **One** who formed us in our mother's womb, and anointed us, clearly has a plan and a purpose for us. Our Heavenly Father, the Creator of Heaven and earth, created us in His image. He gave us our true identity and purpose. Our manufacturer's manual is the "BIBLE".

Basic Instructions Before Leaving Earth!!

Many times, when we are faced with adversity or transitions in life we waste so much of our time seeking answers from well-meaning but misguided individuals. There are many "self-help" books that suggest that looking within ourselves to find purpose is the key to fulfilling our destiny. However, I beg to differ; Being that we were not self- created" we can never find the full purpose of our creation within of us.

Paul said... But life is worth nothing unless I use it for doing the work "assigned me" by the Lord Jesus—the work of telling others the Good News about God's mighty kindness and love (Acts 20:24). He knew that God created him with a designated purpose and his pursuit for anything other than that was worthless. He stood on the Word of his Maker... his Creator. He was confident in his position as a royal priesthood, called and chosen by God. He knew that as long as he followed orders from his

Creator, he would complete his assignment...
fulfilling God's purpose... following God's plan.
God's full purpose and plan for our lives is
found in the Bible... "The Manufacturer's
Manual".

The LORD Gives Jeremiah a Message for His People:

⁴The LORD spoke his word to me, ⁵"Before I formed you in the womb, I knew you. Before you were born, I set you apart for my holy purpose. I appointed you to be a prophet to the nations."
⁶I, Jeremiah, said, "Almighty LORD, I do not know how to speak. I am only a boy!" ⁷But the LORD said to me, "Don't say that you are only a boy. You will go wherever I send you. You will say whatever I command you to say. ⁸Don't be afraid of people. I am with you, and I will rescue you," declares the LORD. ⁹Then the LORD stretched out his hand and touched my mouth. The LORD said to me, "Now I have put my words in your mouth. ¹⁰Today I have put you in charge of nations and kingdoms. You will uproot and tear down. You will destroy and overthrow. You will build and plant."

Jeremiah 1:4-10 (GW)

In these scriptures, the Lord had given Jeremiah his identity and his purpose before he was ever formed in his mother's womb. The one who created him (the manufacturer) told him who he was and what he was created to do. Initially, Jeremiah was fearful because he didn't see himself as God saw him. Fear comes when we see ourselves less than…. He saw himself as a boy but the Lord called him a Prophet to the Nations… Just as God had a plan and purpose for Jeremiah, He has one for you and me. Myles Munroe said… "Your existence is evidence that this generation needs something that your life contains." This means that everybody has a purpose and **the purpose precedes the person**.

There are many scriptures in the Old Testament that predicted the coming of and the purpose of Jesus. Jesus' purpose preceded His entrance. Jesus knew His purpose and He refused to allow anything or anyone to interfere with His assignment.

For to us a child is born. To us a son is given; and the government will be on his shoulders. His name will be called Wonderful, Counselor, Mighty God, Everlasting Father, Prince of Peace.

Isaiah 9:6 (WEB)

As a young boy (12 years- old), Jesus was focused on carrying out the mission that God the Father had given Him; he was confident in the one who sent Him. Jesus knew His true identity and He withstood every distraction.

- (Read and meditate on Luke 2:41-50)

As we move toward our destiny, our ETA (estimated time of arrival) can be delayed if we are led by fear and not faith. *Fear blinds potential and paralyses purpose.*

Let it be known that we have an adversary that wants to plant seeds of fear and doubt in our spirit; he wants to rob us of knowing our true identity (Heirs of God and a joint heir with Christ). We must refuse to allow the fear tactics of the enemy to cause us to forfeit our royal inheritance. We must understand that there is a strong magnetic force between knowing our true identity and walking in our purpose.

When an object is correctly identified, knowing the purpose for its use is clear. For instance, I have used the bottom of my shoes as a hammer (to assist with nailing or tacking something, when a hammer was not readily available) and I have also used my shoes to smash pesky insects. However, my shoes are more effective when used for what they were created for...... "WALKING" ... What am I saying? I am saying that when we get a revelation of our true identity and the purpose in which we were created, we are more effective in our God-given assignments.

God's gifts are without repentance. Romans 11:29 Message translation says it best... "God's gifts and God's call are under full warranty- never canceled, never rescinded. The delays and detours that we encounter on the road to destiny have less to do with God changing His mind and more to do with our disobedience.

"He had and still has a plan for you!"

Be sober and self-controlled. Be watchful. Your adversary, the devil, walks around like a roaring lion, seeking whom he may devour.

1 Peter 5:8 (WEB)

For I know the plans *and* thoughts that I have for you,' says the LORD, 'plans for peace *and* well-being and not for disaster to give you a future and a hope.

Jeremiah 29:11(AMP)

And [that you may come] to know[practically, through personal experience] the love of Christ which far surpasses [mere] knowledge [without experience], that you may be filled up [throughout your being] to all the fullness of God [so that you may have the richest experience of God's presence in your lives, completely filled and flooded with God Himself].

Ephesians 3:19

OBEDIENCE BRINGS THE BLESSING...!

CHAPTER 2

TRUE IDENTITY

And he has identified us as his own by placing the Holy Spirit in our hearts as the first installment that guarantees everything he has promised us.

2 Corinthians 1:22(NLT)

There is a place deep inside of us that knows

when things are true. It's when you know, that

you know. I call it knowing within your

"knower". Everybody has a "knower". It's that

place of confidence deep down in your gut.

When you know, in your knower, who you are,

and whose you are, no devil in hell can stop you.

Knowing who we are in the natural (our name,

our parents, siblings etc.) has a purpose but knowing who we are spiritually gives us purpose. Our purpose is birthed out of knowing our true identity. Our self-fulfilling expectations, earthly titles, and positions do not identify us. Earthly titles are as sinking sand. There is no stability in seeking to find our identity outside of Christ because it leads to disappointment. Our true identity in Christ is solid.

There are many scriptures in the bible that tells us who we are and who we belong to. One that was eye opening for me is 2 Corinthians 1:22. If there was such a thing as a "Christian I.D. card", I believe that 2 Corinthians 1:22 would be printed on the front of it. This scripture reveals to "us" who we are and it also guarantees our position...100% guarantee.

As we confidently walk in our true identity there should be a transformation.   So, you ask, "what type of transformation?" I stated earlier that 2 Corinthians 1:22 reveals to us who we are, but, the life we live reveals to "others" whose we are. In other words, we can only convince others that we know our true identity by how we live... how we respond to the issues of life. Who we are in a crisis will quickly bring clarity to whether we truly know "in our knower" who we are in Christ...Our "TRUE IDENTITY". It has been through developing a relationship with God that I gained this revelation.

Developing a relationship with God is an active and constant process. As we receive impartation through our relationship with Him there should

be some resemblance...we should begin to

resemble God. Those we receive from, we will

resemble...good or bad... It's called DNA.

When I was a young girl my identity was

connected to my parents. People would never

really ask my name; they would say things like,

"hey...are you Mr. Minor's daughter or Pastor

Minor's daughter?   In the school setting,

starting at kindergarten through the 8th grade, I

was identified by my father; He was my daddy

and my Assistant Principal (ouch)...   Anytime I

was away from the school environment, I was

then identified by my Mom. People would say...

"You must be Orleana Minor's daughter because

you look just like her". The

places I could go where people did no

I was and who I belonged to. Remember wh

said earlier about "resemblance" …. Note to

self… "our fruit reveals the tree we are from".

Any time my sisters and I left home, my dad

always reminded us that we represented him. I

believe that is how Father God is with us. He

wants us to know in our "knower" that our true

identity is in Him through Christ Jesus. We are

Heaven's earthly representatives. When we

accept Jesus Christ as our Lord and Savior, we

don't lose our true self… we become our "TRUE

SELF" …. It is imperative that we know this

truth!!

WE ARE WHO HE SAYS WE ARE…!

s one beloved
**lf. Every other
usion."**

: Abba's Child

V) says "Whoever is a

 new creation. The old way

of livi.   peared. A new way of living

has come into existence". So, what is included in

this new way of living?   This new way of living

must refuse to chase after the desires of the

flesh and begin to chase after the things that will

glorify God. As a new creation, walking in our

true identity, we should desire to bring God

glory in all areas of our life. Walking in our true

identity does not mean that we will not face

adversity; it means that when we face trials and

tribulations we respond in faith, not fear.

Stolen Identity

Without knowing God's Word, his promises, and purpose for us, we can find ourselves having our identity stolen. How is this possible? The answer is...the "fear factor". Fear has the potential of distorting our perception of whether we truly have a purpose. Fear and anxiety will bring your destiny journey to a screeching halt. A life filled with fear and anxiety diminishes our focus on God's ability to carry out His purpose through us.

"Failing faith will weaken the pursuit of purpose every time".

The bible tells us in Ephesians 6 that there is armor available to protect us against the schemes of the enemy; his tricks and traps are not blatant, they are actually very subtle. Afew of his subtle schemes are: issues on the job, car problems, and relationship problems... Don't get it twisted... he is not trying to rob you of your job...he doesn't want to work. He is not trying to take your car... he can't drive it. He's not trying to steal your house...he can't live in it... The enemy is trying to rob you of your **faith**.   Satan wants you to lose hope, and leave you without a sense of purpose.   Jesus warned Peter that satan wanted to sift him as wheat (meaning he wanted to weaken Peter's faith); So, I'm here to warn you as well…. **"The enemy wants to weaken your faith…"**

The TLB translation of Hebrew 11:1 defines faith

you look just like her". There were not many places I could go where people did not know who I was and who I belonged to. Remember whatI said earlier about "resemblance" …. Note to self… "our fruit reveals the tree we are from".

Any time my sisters and I left home, my dad always reminded us that we represented him. I believe that is how Father God is with us. He wants us to know in our "knower" that our true identity is in Him through Christ Jesus. We are Heaven's earthly representatives. When we accept Jesus Christ as our Lord and Savior, we don't lose our true self… we become our "TRUE SELF" …. It is imperative that we know this truth!!

WE ARE WHO HE SAYS WE ARE…!

"Define yourself radically as one beloved by God. This is the true self. Every other identity is an illusion."

–Brennan Manning: Abba's Child

2 Corinthians 5:17 (GW) says "Whoever is a believer in Christ is a new creation. The old way of living has disappeared. A new way of living has come into existence". So, what is included in this new way of living? This new way of living must refuse to chase after the desires of the flesh and begin to chase after the things that will glorify God. As a new creation, walking in our true identity, we should desire to bring God glory in all areas of our life. Walking in our true identity does not mean that we will not face adversity; it means that when we face trials and tribulations we respond in faith, not fear.

in such a way that it makes the enemy afraid of us. It says that "faith is the confident assurance that something we want is going to happen; It is the certainty that what we hope for is waiting for us, even though we cannot see it up ahead". Hallelujah!! So, hold on to your faith and don't let go!!! We must continue to hold firmly to our declaration of faith. The one who made the promise is faithful (Hebrews 10:23). Faith is the bridge between where you are today and your destiny. The revelation knowledge found in the Word of God builds your faith to fulfill your purpose. Faith comes by hearing, and hearing, and hearing, the Word of God. No Word... No Faith. Faithlessness can lead straight into an identity crisis.

Consequently, faith comes from hearing the message, and the message is heard through the word about Christ.

Romans 10:17(NIV)

32"Simon, Simon (Peter), listen! Satan has demanded *permission* to sift [all of] you like grain; 32but I have prayed [especially] for you [Peter], that your faith [and confidence in Me] may not fail;

Luke 22:31-32 (AMP)

Let us seize *and* hold tightly the confession of our hope without wavering, for He who promised is reliable *and* trustworthy *and* faithful [to His word];

Hebrews 10:23 (AMP)

Describe what 2 Corinthians 1:22 means to you?

_____

_____

_____

_____

_____

Has there been a time in your life that you felt you had lost your identity? _____

How did you get back on track?

_____

_____

_____

_____

_____

Has a spirit of fear hindered you from pursuing your purpose?

_____

_____

_____

_____

_____

_____

What has been revealed to you since reading this chapter?

_____

_____

_____

_____

_____

_____

_____

_____

_____

_____

_____

_____

_____

_____

_____

CHAPTER 3

IDENTITY CRISIS

Life is filled with transitions from the cradle to the grave. Not having a clear revelation of your self-worth, apart from those you are connected to can lead to a crisis. This is my definition of identity crisis.

My husband and our children are movie buffs. They love going to the movies. I am more of a "watch it when it comes on TV" kind-of girl. One of my favorite movies is "Identity Theft" with Melissa McCarthy. She is one of the funniest actresses around. In this particular movie, she is

involved in an identity theft ring with some
pretty dangerous criminals. She did not become
involved with the criminals because she was
seeking riches; she became involved with them
because she was seeking inclusion...identity.
Although she was stealing and cloning the
identity of others, she was actually seeking her
own. She wasn't sure where she fit in life.

Well, I hope by now you've seen the movie..."
Spoiler Alert Ahead" .... It was toward the end of
the movie that I gained a true revelation. Her
criminal behavior had nothing to do with
possessing fortune or fame, but it had

everything to do with her self-worth. She was
enthralled by the attention she received from

those she worked with (though they were very corrupt individuals). She was seeking to be affirmed; she wanted their acceptance. Her deep need for acceptance was rooted out of her childhood trauma. She did not know her birth parents and neither did she know her birth name. Her childhood pains left her with a void and she used stealing, spending, or any other criminal behavior to ease her pain. She was willing to fill her emptiness with bad company for the sake of IDENTITY... Does this sound familiar?

Do not be misled: "Bad company corrupts good character."
1 Corinthians 15:33(NIV)

This woman had no perception of her true

identity so she pursued the identity of others.

The thievery was birthed out of her own lack of self-worth, low self-esteem, and a lack of purpose.

At the very end of the movie the character was presented with her birth name. In my mind's eye, I can see how having knowledge of her family origin may have given her closure, but it did not give her "PURPOSE".

In this chapter, I described scenes from a movie; however, we all know that this happens to many people, in real life, every day.

Just as I stated earlier, knowing who we are physically (our family name etc.) has "a purpose" but knowing our true identity in Christ, "gives us purpose".

The life of this character could have been different if she had only known who she was in Christ. Well, I didn't write the movie, but indeed, it was a movie filled with great revelation. The title of the movie is Identity Theft; however, it could have been titled, "IDENTITY CRISIS..." I believe an identity "crisis" can occur any time you are faced with a challenge to your sense of self. For example, my husband has the opportunity to speak to youth groups and organizations about leadership. He usually poses the question, "are you an eagle or a chicken"? He then shares a story about a chicken that found an eagle's egg and when the baby eagle hatched, the "mother chicken" began to impart its limitations upon the "baby eagle". The baby eagle was not aware if it's true identity…. The eagle identified itself by those it was surrounded by…chickens!!! The lack of knowing its true identity led to it wandering around out of place…. walking, instead of flying. As my parents always said, "the company you keep, can help you, or hurt you". Any time we adopt the limitations of others as our own, we are in an identity crisis.

For many years, my identity was very connected to my parents. As I transitioned from one setting to the next, from one school to the next, I found it very challenging to find my place. I was lost in the crowd. I had an identity crisis.

Oxford Dictionaries defines an identity crisis as a period of uncertainty and confusion in which a person's sense of identity becomes insecure, typically, due to a change in their expected aims or role in society. Psychologist Erik Erikson's definition of an identity crisis focuses mainly on the adolescence period of life. I believe an identity crisis can occur at any age, or stage of life (far beyond adolescence). Wherever there is a transition, an identity crisis can occur.

Did you experience a childhood trauma that left you broken and feeling empty? _____

How have you dealt with it?

_____

_____

_____

_____

Has there been a season in your life that you were not comfortable in your own skin?

_____

_____

_____

_____

_____

If so, how did you get back on track?

_____

_____

_____

_____

_____

Have you ever found yourself more interested or consumed with someone else's life one lifestyle?

_____

_____

_____

_____

CHAPTER 4

TRANSITIONS

There is an old hymn that I remembered singing

in church as a young girl titled, "Hold to God's

Unchanging Hand". The first line of the hymn

says..." "Time is filled with swift transition"

...Those lyrics meant nothing to me as a child,

but now I get it. Transition is like change... it is

fast and inevitable.   As long as we have breath

in our body, we will face transitions. It is

imperative that we seek God's Word to find out

what He says about us... especially during the

transitions. His word and His promises is the

anchor that holds us steady during the storms

and the swift transitions.

My identity struggles were more challenging during my young adult years as opposed to my early school age years. The shift from home to college was not as smooth I had imagined. It was during my college years that I became uncertain about who I was, and where I belonged.... I often pondered the question in my mind... who am I and where do I fit?   It wasn't until later in life that I began to understand this... "If you don't know who you are, there is no way to know where you fit". Many times, I felt like a square peg trying to fit in a round opening. Once again, in a new setting I was feeling like a misfit... feeling totally out of place. I was very aware of whom my daddy said I was; however, I had no idea who my Heavenly Father said I was.

The identity I gained from my parents was not enough to carry me through life. Knowing our family origin has a purpose but it does not give us purpose. It is our true identity in Christ that gives us purpose. We must remind ourselves of this truth daily!!!

Knowing who we are in Christ is the key to our true identity and being aware of this determines how we handle transitions in life. I've come to the realization that my relationship with my earthly father was strong because of the time we spent together. So, in order for me to remain confident in who my Heavenly Father says I am,

I must spend time with Him. This would become the main ingredient in strengthening any "relationship". I grew up in the church, going through the motions (an outward performance but no inward change). I learned religious protocol, but I was malnourished in my own personal relationship with God. Along the way, I missed some steps. I was getting up Sunday after Sunday, going to church, just to check the block. There is an old saying.... you can lead a horse to water but you can't make him drink.... Well, I was led to church, but I did not drink. I had no understanding that drinking from the well of the Word of God would be necessary for my spiritual development. Due to lack of developing my own relationship, I had no clue who God created me to be (besides "my daddy's little girl"). That unawareness caused me to allow external forces to distort my view of myself... driving me very close to ruining my life completely. Why? I failed to recognize the authenticity of my creation.

My people are ruined because they don't know what's right or true.

Hosea 4:6(MSG)

People are destroyed by the lack of knowledge. My knowledge was not limited due to not being taught. My knowledge was limited due to my lack of willingness to listen to and obey God's word. Now you're probably wondering, "how was I a pastor's daughter and not have a clue who I was spiritually"? All religion... No relationship.

Moving from the familiar to the unfamiliar can leave you feeling "some kind of way". I knew who I was physically (on the outside), but I had no clue who I was spiritually (on the inside). I didn't know my true purpose. Somewhere along the way I went through the motions thinking that that was enough. I had no daily communication with Father God. My outer crust was very well done but my inside was raw... uncooked. This is a perfect recipe for an IDENTITY CRISIS...cooked on the outside, raw on the inside. My husband has a saying "when the student is ready, the teacher will appear". I was not ready until I began to face "LIFE" without being connected to my parents.

It wasn't my parent's responsibility to develop "MY" relationship. They were not to blame for my lack of spiritual development....

"YOU CAN'T BLAME YOUR WAY INTO A BETTER FUTURE"
-Andy Stanley

My parents were responsible for laying the foundation (and they did that), but I was responsible for my own growth. I realized that my spiritual growth was connected to "my" appetite... "my" hunger. The promise of Matthew 5:6 became very real to me... "Blessed are those who hunger and thirst after righteousness... they shall be filled". It was then that my soul became hungry, and my growth became intentional.

"Knowing our physical identity (family name/roots; heritage) has "a" purpose but knowing our identity in Christ "gives us purpose".

-Renee Johnson

"Change is inevitable and growth is
intentional..."

-John C. Maxwell

Have there been any relationships or situations
that you were drawn to due to a lack of self-esteem
or self-worth?

_____

_____

If so, in retrospect, what did you learn about
yourself once you were removed from the
situation/relationship?

_____

_____

_____

Have you ever found yourself getting caught up in
life's issues and compromised your relationship
with God? If so, how did you get back on track?
Explain.

_____

_____

_____

Have you ever lost you way in one of life's transitions?   Explain.

_____

_____

_____

Are you intentional in the area of your spiritual growth?   Explain.

_____

_____

_____

_____

_____

JOURNAL

_____

_____

_____

_____

_____

_____

_____

CHAPTER 5

THE HUNGRY SOUL

HUNGER IS A POWERFUL FORCE...

Taking hold of, and maintaining our royal
position as believers is predicated on our
commitment to feeding the seeds of purpose
that Father God planted within us. Our level of
hunger determines our level of growth. The
hunger is connected to our relationship with the
HOLY SPIRIT. The word promises that the Lord
satisfies the longing soul, and the hungry soul
He fills with good things (Psalms 107:9).

Our soul is our mind, our will, and our emotions.
When our soul becomes thirsty, it can only be

satisfied by Living Water (the Holy Spirit). This Living Water brings life to our mortal bodies and it becomes the wind that pushes us on a pursuit for purpose. It has taken me many years to come to the revelation that my hunger is connected to my purpose... royal destiny!!

Hunger

According to THEFREEDICTIONARY.com, hunger is defined as "strong desire or need for food; the discomfort, weakness, or pain caused by a prolonged lack of food, "or a strong desire or craving". This definition captures the true meaning of hunger ... spiritually and physically (I'll come back to the parallel later). Our body needs fuel to function. When we lack the necessary fuel to function, a signal is sent to the brain to alert us to eat or drink something. The longer one goes without nourishment, the weaker the body becomes. When I think of being hungry, I envision the dashboard in a car. The dash indicator alerts the driver that fuel is needed. The fuel indicator detects how much fuel you have...as it runs low, the indicator informs you. Cars often perform differently when running out of gas. When running very low on fuel, the vehicle might begin to sputter; if running totally out of gas, possible engine damage could occur. All of these things can be avoided by simply paying attention to the dash indicator. I believe that we possess a spiritual dash indicator within us.

Allow me to go further... When we lose our focus, and respond to adverse situations, and circumstance, with a chaotic, fearful spirit, our spiritual dash indicator is letting us know that we're running low on fuel. Do you pay attention to your dash indicator?

I know the importance of never allowing your tank to get empty. Personally, I am very attentive to my dash indicator and I never allow my car to get below quarter....1/4 tank. When my husband and I travel, I always ask the question..." should we fill-up again?" I prefer to see the fuel level on full. I don't want to take any chances on running low or running out of gas; and, so it is, in the Spirit. I don't want to take the risk of running low or running out of spiritual food. The reward outweighs the risk...Our destiny is predicated on our level of hunger... our appetite.

A loss of hunger and lack of spiritual fuel is the beginning of death. You might ask death of what? - Death of your dreams, your vision, your passion, and your purpose.

The Power of Hunger

Hunger is one of the strongest motivators in animals and is the driving force of their behavior. I would say the same is true for humans as well. Our hunger and our appetite is the driving force of the decisions we make in life. Hunger will determine the road we take... ultimately, determining our destiny. Lack of hunger and being hungry for the wrong things can be unhealthy (physically and spiritually). If there is no hunger inside.... your seed, your vision, your dreams will surely die: If one satisfies hunger with the wrong things, the same is possible.

The parallels of physical and spiritual hunger are very similar. For example, a newborn comes out of the womb hungry. His/her first cry out of the womb expresses the "power of hunger". We come in this world with an appetite for food, comfort, attention, and love. When a baby wants milk, there is nothing else that can satisfy him/her... the pacifier might help for a moment, but it won't satisfy the hunger.

It is at this infant stage that the behavior to

satisfy a need is developed. This would be driving force that determines the road we take...decisions we make...our destiny....

Our Divine Destiny

There are a number of conditions that can lead to a decrease in one's **appetite**. In mostcases, however, one's appetite will return to normal once the proper nutrition is provided. For instance, with newborns, if their appetite decreases, the doctor and the child's mother might become very concerned... Why? As the baby's appetite grows, the baby should grow proportionally to that hunger. If this does not occur, the baby's loss of appetite and lack of desire for food can lead to death!!!!!!

In an adult patient, if he/she is not hungry and has no appetite, the physician will usually request a panel of test to see what is causing the loss of appetite. Nine out of ten times, the loss of appetite is due to an imbalance in the body or a lack of proper nutrients necessary to sustain the body's proper functioning. Without the proper nutrition, a decline in health is inevitable. This decline could possibly lead to death. Frequently, doctors will prescribe the drug, **Megace**. Megace is used to stir up hunger and increase the desire for food... it is an appetite stimulant. This drug is given with the hope of increasing one's appetite, which will subsequently lead to restoration and healing....

No hunger, no nutrition, no growth!!!!

The absence of hunger can lead to a

decline in health and possibly death!!!!!

God created hunger for a purpose....it is

necessary to have a healthy appetite both

spiritually and physically. Why? Because

whatever you feed, will grow. Just as Megace is

an appetite stimulant for the physical man;

The Holy Spirit is the appetite stimulant for the

spiritual man. The Holy Spirit is our Helper or

Counselor... always available to empower us to

complete our divine appointments. Therefore, it

is imperative to have a relationship with the

Holy Spirit. Knowing our true identity and our

royal position in Christ is dependent on this relationship. The Holy Spirit stirs up a hunger or an appetite for wisdom, revelation, and direction…. He causes us to inquisitively dig for answers as our appetite to walk with Him grows. When the Holy Spirit reveals something to us in the spirit; it stirs up a hunger…. The stronger our appetite, the more we eat… The more we eat, the more fuel we have for the journey ahead.

The Holy Spirit stirs up a hunger in us because He knows what's awaiting us beyond the lights. He will never stir up a hunger that He can't satisfy. Every time He stirs up a hunger, He fills it……. He satisfies… He empowers….

"The Holy Spirit Is Fuel for Faith"

1"O God, you are my God. Early will I seek you. My soul thirsts for You. My flesh longs for You in a dry and thirsty land where there is no water. 2So, I have looked for You in the sanctuary, to see Your power and Your glory"

Psalm 63: 1-2 (NKJV)

Blessed are those who hunger and thirst for righteousness, for they shall be filled.

Matthew 5:6 (NKJV)

When you are passionate about something, you are drawn to those with the same hunger. It is important to stay connected with hungry people (people that have an appetite for purpose and greatness). **Remember, the level of your hunger will determine your next blessing!!** The fuel needed to pursue your destiny will be determined by your level of hunger. Have you experienced unsatisfied cravings lately? Do you know what your spirit is craving? Psalm 63:5 says..." You satisfy me more than the richest feast." The Bread of Life...Living Water" will always satisfy the hungry soul.

Some signs of Spiritual hunger:

- Discontentment
- Restless nights
- Frustration on your job
- Activities that you used to enjoy, aren't fun anymore...

Just as in the spiritual, it is so in the natural... the longer you go without nourishment, the less hungry you become. As soon as we begin to eat, read, and learn more about Jesus, and what His resurrecting power means to us as believers, the more our spiritual appetite increases.

An increase in our spiritual appetite is the magnet that draws us to our divine purpose.

The seed of purpose was planted in us before the foundations of the earth. It is our responsibility to feed our seeds. We must keep an aching and nagging appetite in order to consume all God has for us to know and to become. Our inheritance awaits us. The Holy Spirit never grows old or irrelevant which means you can never stop learning and receiving revelations regarding His divine plan and purpose. God's Word promises to satisfy the hungry with good things. So, allow me to encourage you with this...We must seek the Word of God and have a constant refilling of the Holy Spirit to gain wisdom for every situation. Along with a constant filling, the following things are necessary for growth:

- **Keep a healthy appetite**
- **Feed your seed**
- **Don't let your fuel run low**
- **Stay connected to hungry people**

PSALM 107:9...For He satisfies the longing soul, and the hungry soul he fills with good things.

How often are you feeding your spiritual body?

_____

_____

_____

Do you have a circle of spiritually, hungry friends?

_____

_____

Read Mark 2:1-12

FEED YOUR DREAMS

By Renee Johnson

You have to feed your dreams,
or they will never grow.

The appetite of your dreams;
determine where you go.

Without vision as people we can never thrive;
You got to feed my dreams for them to stay
alive...

You need to write it on tablets
Just to make it plain;

So, everybody that reads it
would dare to stay the same;

Don't allow your dream bank to run low;
Without deposits your dream bank will never
grow...
Without vision as people we can never thrive;

You got to feed your dreams for them to stay alive...

A dream without a plan is a hallucination;

To talk of dreams with no plans is just a conversation...

When you feed your dreams, your dreams will feed you back;

Expand the size of your dreams and never live in lack...

Big dreams and hard work go hand in hand;

You can't fulfill your dreams without a master plan...

The hunger pain of your dreams will truly tell the story;

Infuse your dream with faith and wait to see the glory.

CHAPTER 6

THE POWER OF WORDS

"I am who God says I am, and I can do what God says I can do"!

Pastor Mark Hankins has many profound quotes. One of my favorites is....

"Your confession precedes your possession". My Pastor, Caleb Moran, preached a sermon titled "Your Future Is Listening". Though both phrases involved only a few words, the message from each is filled with powerful revelation... Our words have power, and if we are not careful, we can speak the wrong words and possess something we do not want. Words have power!!!

What you plant or allow to be planted will grow. It is imperative that we pay close attention to the things that we allow to come out of our mouths, and the things we allow to be planted in our minds!! Words have creative power. Negative words have the power to produce negative thoughts... Positive words have the power to produce positive thoughts. It is possible to change our environment, (be it work, home, hair salon, etc...) with the words we speak into the atmosphere. It is also possible to allow words spoken in our environment to change us...!!!!!

Have you ever attended a sporting event (basketball... football) and the cheerleaders motioned for the crowd to get involved?

It seems that as the crowd gets involved and chants become louder, the performance of their team becomes more intense.... One of our sons played basketball on a couple of different levels. When he played basketball in high school, one chant we often yelled was "DEFENSE" ... The crowd would yell "defense" and I would scream in between "TAKE THE BALL". It wasn't too long before our team would cause a turnover, steal the ball, and score. The cheers and chants encouraged our team to persevere while psychologically intimating the opposing team.

On one hand, the words/cheers planted a seed of victory in one team and then planted a seed of defeat in another. Wow! Look at the power of words. Words are seeds... be careful where you plant them, and where you allow them to grow.

We must use our God-given authority to change what we see by what we say. God's word lets us know that we are victorious regardless of the opinion or voices of the crowd. When we believe we are who God says we are, it doesn't matter what others think of us or say about us. When we believe that God's Word is truth, we become confident He is the one who began this good work in us, and He won't stop before it is complete. That confidence brings boldness. There is a reward connected to our confidence; don't throw it away (Hebrews 10:35-36).

Speak Life!!!!!

Death and life are in the power of the tongue, And those who love it *and* indulge it will eat its fruit *and* bear the consequences of their words.

-Proverbs 18:21 (AMP)

"Be strong. Take courage. Don't be intimidated. Don't give them a second thought because God, your God, is striding ahead of you. He's right there with you. He won't let you down; he won't leave you." .....,

-Deuteronomy 31:6 (MSG)

From the beginning, I revealed the end. From long ago I told you things that had not yet happened, saying, "My plan will stand, and I'll do everything I intended to do."

-Isaiah 46:10 (GW)

Words have power. The words you speak and the words you listen to can determine your destiny. I choose to listen to and speak God's Word into and over my life.

Confession Leads to Possession

Luke 6:45 (NLT) says "what you say flows from what is in your heart". One might ask the question, "How do words enter our heart"? Well, the heart is fed through hearing and seeing. What we listen to, and what we watch, feed our heart. Therefore, it would be very difficult to rise up and confess God's Word and possess God's promises, if we have not been listening or watching the things that are in line with His Word. How many times have you adopted clichés or sayings of others as our own? Why does this happen? This can be traced back to things our ears have heard, and things our eyes have seen. Proverbs 18:21 says "death and life are in the power of the tongue".

If you want to rise up and receive life, you must speak life. The power is in your tongue... those who love it will eat its fruits. "Your future is listening".

Say What You Want to See...

PTSD is an acronym that is very prevalent in our society today. Coming from a military background, PTSD is heard often. Well as you know, the meaning of PTSD is **Post-Traumatic Stress Disorder.** The **National Institute of Mental Health** defines PTSD as a disorder that develops in some people who have experienced a shocking, scary, or dangerous event. **NIMH** also listed various factors or triggers that lead to PTSD...

Some factors that increase risk for PTSD include:

- **Living through dangerous events and traumas**
- **Getting hurt**
- **Seeing another person hurt, or seeing a dead body**
- **Childhood trauma**
- **Feeling horror, helplessness, or extreme fear**
- **Having little or no social support after the event**
- **Dealing with extra stress after the event, such as loss of a loved one, pain and injury, or loss of a job or home**

After studying the information on PTSD, I found another acronym that I had not previously seen or heard... **"PTG"**. PTG is Post-Traumatic Growth. I had no idea that this existed.

Revelation... we can really perish for the lack of

knowledge. Who knew that there could be such a thing as Post-Traumatic Growth after a traumatic experience? **"We can rise up out of a mess with a life changing message."**

UNC-Charlotte Post-Traumatic Growth Research Group of the Department of Psychology defines PTG as follows: It is "positive change" experienced as a result of the struggle with a major life crisis or a traumatic event. Although we coined the term *post-traumatic growth*, the idea that human beings can be changed by their encounters with life challenges, sometimes in radically positive ways, is not new.

What forms does post-traumatic growth take?

Post-traumatic growth tends to occur in five general areas when:

1) People who must face major life crises develop a sense that new opportunities have emerged from the struggle, opening up possibilities that were not present before.

2) There is a change in relationships with others. Some people experience closer relationships with some specific people, and they can also experience an increased sense of connection to others who suffer.

3) There is an increased sense of one's own strength – *"if I lived through that, I can face anything"*.

4) One has a greater appreciation for life in general.

5) Some individuals experience a deepening of their spiritual lives; <u>however</u>, this deepening can also involve a significant change in one's belief system.

It was after studying this information by UNC-Charlotte that PTSG was downloaded in my spirit…. "Post-Traumatic Spiritual Growth" or "PTSG". I realized that the same trauma that caused a stress disorder in some could also cause spiritual growth in another. James 1:2-4 says... "Consider it nothing but joy, my brothers and sisters, whenever you fall into various trials. [3]Be assured that the testing of your faith [through experience] produces endurance [leading to spiritual maturity, and inner peace].

[4]And let endurance have its perfect result and do a thorough work, so that you may be perfect and completely developed [in your faith], lacking in nothing". This scripture means that it is possible to become stronger after trials. It is true; positive spiritual growth can come after adversity. We need both sunshine and rain to grow. **John Maxwell says, "You are either ripening or rotting" And often times the**

"ripening' comes as a result of adversity and tough times.

If the power of life and death is in the tongue, I believe we should speak what we want to see... Why? Our future is listening.

Our perception and the words that we speak play a big role in reaching our royal destiny. If we can change our perception, we can change our reality. The power of life and death is in our tongue. When we go through the valley of the shadow of death our outcome will depend upon the power of our words. What you confess, you will possess...Change what you say and change what you see. What will you confess in your lion's den...?   PTSD or PTSG??

²²Jesus said to them, "Have faith in God! ²³I can guarantee this truth: This is what will be done for someone who doesn't doubt but believes what he says will happen: He can say to this mountain, 'Be uprooted and thrown into the sea,' and it will be done for him.

Mark 11:22-23 (GW)

But I thank God, who always leads us in victory because of Christ. Wherever we go, God uses us to make clear what it means to know Christ. ......
2 Corinthians 2:14(GW)

Now God has us where he wants us, with all the time in this world and the next to shower grace and kindness upon us in Christ Jesus. Saving is all his idea, and all his work. All we do is trust him enough to let him do it. It's God's gift from start to finish! We don't play the major role. If we did, we'd probably go around bragging that we'd done the whole thing! No, we neither make nor save ourselves. God does both the making and saving. He creates each of us by Christ Jesus to join him in the work he does, the good work he has gotten ready for us to do, work we had better be doing.
Ephesians 2:7-10 (MSG)

I AM....

I am created In God's likeness.
Ephesians 4:24

I am a whole new person with a whole new life...
2 Corinthians 5:17

I am God's Incredible work of art; His workmanship.
Ephesians 2:10

I am totally and completely forgiven.
1 John 1:9

I am spiritually alive.
Ephesians 2:5

I am a citizen of Heaven.
Philippians 3:20

I am God's disciple-maker.
Matthew 28:19

I am the light of the world.
Matthew 5:14

I am greatly loved.
Romans 5:8

I am triumphant.
2 Corinthians 2:14

I am a child of God.
Galatians 3:26

71

MAKE YOUR CONFESSION PLAIN......

_____

_____

_____

_____

_____

_____

_____

_____

_____

*AND WHO KNOWS BUT THAT YOU HAVE
COME TO YOUR ROYAL POSITION FOR
SUCH A TIME AS THIS?"
ESTHER 4:14 (NIV)*

CHAPTER 7

HOW GOD SEES ME

How God sees me? This is a question that I pondered for many years. To be honest, for a long time, I never really knew how He saw me. I didn't understand that He saw me as daughter. I understood God to be big, majestic, almighty and all-powerful but I didn't fully understand Him as **DADDY GOD**... **ABBA FATHER** (Galatians 4:6). I did not have the full understanding of Him as a Loving Father.

My faulty perception of myself skewed my vision of Our Heavenly Father. Allow me to put it in layman's terms... I saw Father God as the employer; I saw myself as an employee. I was clueless regarding my inheritance as an heir of the company! I had no knowledge of my rights and privileges as a daughter of the King.

And because we are his children, God has sent the Spirit of his Son into our hearts, prompting us to call out, "Abba, Father".
Galatians 4:6 (NLT)

My husband (Terry) and I have a blended family (4 boys and 1 girl). I call it "a family of one" ... many members, one family. When Terry and I met, I was a single parent of an eight-year-old (Justin). We were married a few months after we met (that's another story within itself). As soon as we were married my husband stated that he wanted to adopt my son. He said that he wanted to give Justin his last name and all of the

benefits that would be available to any

biological child. From the beginning of our

marriage, Terry saw Justin as son. Justin

received every physical, emotional,

financial, and spiritual privilege that came

with being the son of Terry Johnson. Just as

there were benefits connected with that

physical adoption, we have benefits that are

connected with our spiritual adoption. The

benefit package that is attached to our

position as sons and daughters of the "Most

High" exceeds any corporate benefit

package. When we were adopted into the

family of God, we had immediate access to

every spiritual blessing as a joint heir with

Christ. Daddy God will withhold no good

thing from us. He sees us as sons and

daughters... **Royalty**.

³Blessed be the God and Father of our Lord Jesus Christ, who has blessed us with every spiritual blessing in the heavenly places in Christ; ⁴even as he chose us in him before the foundation of the world, that we would be holy and without defect before him in love; ⁵having predestined us for adoption as children through Jesus Christ to himself, according to the good pleasure of his desire, ⁶to the praise of the glory of his grace, by which he freely gave us favor in the Beloved, ⁷in whom we have our redemption through his blood, the forgiveness of our trespasses, according to the riches of his grace, ⁸which he made to abound toward us in all wisdom and prudence, ⁹making known to us the mystery of his will, according to his good pleasure which he purposed in him ¹⁰to an administration of the fullness of the times, to sum up all things in Christ, the things in the heavens, and the things on the earth, in him; ¹¹in whom also we were assigned an inheritance, having been foreordained according to the purpose of him

who does all things after the counsel of his will;

Ephesians 1:3-11(WEB)

Many times, we see ourselves through the eyes of imperfections.... lack, hurt, betrayal, abandonment, and rejection. The enemy knows that we were born with a divine purpose. His plan is to taint how we see ourselves. Satan begins imparting deception and lies in our spirit early in life. He uses the lies of hurt, betrayal, and rejection to cause us to lose hope in the promises of God, but little does he know...what he means for evil, God uses it for our good. The story of Joseph in The Old Testament is a good example. The story of Joseph is just one of several revealed in the bible in which the enemy tried to destroy the destiny of a great leader, at a young age. Joseph was 17 years-old when he began to experience rejection and betrayal. But God, being Alpha and Omega, knew the end at the beginning (Genesis 37-50).

As for you, you meant evil against me, <u>BUT GOD</u> meant it for good in order to bring about this present outcome, that many people would be kept alive [as they are this day].
Genesis 50:20 (AMP)

I capitalized and underlined the **"<u>BUT GOD</u>"** for a reason…. Just know that **Victory** comes after every **"<u>BUT GOD</u>"**. Father God always makes it possible through Christ to lead us into victory… (2 Corinthians 2:14 CEV). God saw Joseph victorious from the start and that is how he sees us. He says we are **ROYALTY!!**

I love reading about the woman at the well in John 4. This Samaritan woman in John 4 did not leave the well the same way she came. In her "Well Experience" she had two revelations...her first revelation was how she saw Jesus and the second one was how she saw herself. Being in the presence of God changed her life and it will also change yours. We will never see ourselves until we see ourselves in the presence of God. Being in His presence is the key to opening our eyes and truly knowing how He sees us. In His presence, the Samaritan woman came to grips with the fact that she had to let go of her past, her sin, and her shame. The life she had lived before meeting Jesus could no longer remain.

Upon her awakening, she dropped her pot, her past, and her embarrassment, and shared her "Well Experience "with everyone she met. This was another "BUT GOD" situation where the enemy's intensions failed. Her past would no longer hold her back from her future. She decided to **Rise-Up** and walk in her Divine purpose.

"Arise [from spiritual depression to a new life], shine [be radiant with the glory *and* brilliance of the LORD]; for your light has come, And the glory *and* brilliance of the LORD has risen upon you."

Isaiah 60:1(AMP)

-Read and Meditate on Ephesians 1

-Read and Meditate on Genesis 37-50 and John 4

Do you have a Joseph or a Samaritan Woman story?

_____

_____

_____

_____

_____

_____

_____

_____

_____

_____

Never Changing

Every team needs cheerleaders. Whether it's a sports team, a family, a church family…. we all need cheerleaders. Cheerleaders stand on the sidelines, watching teammates perform, and they scream chants and cheers to encourage their teammates to stay in the fight. Even when the team is losing, I've never seen cheerleaders switch their uniform in the middle of a game to cheer for the opposing team. This reminds me of how Father God is with us... He never changes His mind about us. Even when we're not performing well in this game called life, He still cheers for us, calling us overcomers, more than conquerors, triumphant. Although we get off track, He knows what it takes to get us back on course... He knows how to work things together for our good...

And we know [with great confidence] that God [who is deeply concerned about us] causes all things to work together [as a plan] for good

for those who love God, to those who are called according to His plan *and* purpose.

Romans 8:28 (AMP)

Father God is All Knowing... Omniscient... He is Alpha and Omega... He knows the end at the beginning!!!! The scripture tells us that Gods always leads us into victory, and regardless of what we see; we must believe that "victory is a promise". When we begin to see ourselves the way the Father sees us, we reap the benefits of the revelation. How do you see you?

"How we see ourselves determines the strength of the magnet that draws us to our destiny".
-Renee Johnson

WALKING in VICTORY

Walking in victory starts with "walking by FAITH". Without faith in the truth of the God's word, walking in victory is not possible. We must believe God is who He says He is, and we are who He says we are…. That takes faith. Faith comes by hearing the word of God. You have to know, in your "knower", that at the end of the day, God is working things out on your behalf… (Not for your name sake but for His name sake). His Word never returns empty! The battles we face are battles that He has already won. We must stay in the game, stay focused and never quit. The championship is yours, so don't give up. If God is for you, nothing can stand against you.

"Stay in the fight" …

The full armor needed to win the fight is found in Ephesians 6. The enemy does not want us to know who we are or whose we are. Satan wants to feed us lies about our identity and our inheritance. Ephesians 6:10-17 lays out the strategic defense against the enemy's schemes.

The Armor of God

[10]**Finally, be strong in the Lord, and in the strength of his might.** [11]**Put on the whole armor of God, that you may be able to stand against the wiles of the devil.** [12]**For our wrestling is not against flesh and blood, but against the principalities, against the powers, against the world's rulers of the darkness of this age, and against the spiritual forces of wickedness in the heavenly places.** [13]**Therefore put on the whole armor of God, that you may be able to withstand in the evil day, and, having done all, to stand.** [14]**Stand therefore, having the utility belt of truth buckled around your waist, and having put on the breastplate of righteousness,**

[15]**and having fitted your feet with the preparation of the Good News of peace;** [16]**above all, taking up the shield of faith, with which you will be able to quench all the fiery darts of the evil one.**

¹⁷And take the helmet of salvation, and the sword of the Spirit, which is the word of God; ¹⁸with all prayer and requests, praying at all times in the Spirit, and being watchful to this end in all perseverance and requests for all the saints:

Ephesians 6:10:18(WEB)

Satan's plan is to kill, steal, and destroy, by any means necessary. So, put on your full armor daily. Every piece has a purpose. Satan wants to try and get you to forfeit your Kingdom position...your inheritance. The enemy knows he can never take your place, however, he will use every lie in his arsenal of lies to stop you from standing firm in your position. He is so adamant about tainting your perception of who you are because he already knows who you are. He knows the authority that we have been given through Christ Jesus....

He is afraid that someday you will boldly stand on God's promises and walk in the place of authority. He is afraid that someday you will come into the revelation of your ROYAL POSITION. We are children of the King; Daughters of the King; a royal priesthood; God's masterpiece.

RISE UP and Take Your Place...

YOU ARE CALLED...

YOU ARE CHOSEN...

YOU ARE ROYALTY...

But you are a chosen race, a royal priesthood, a holy nation, a people for God's own possession, that you may proclaim the excellencies of Him who called you out of darkness into His marvelous light;

1 Peter 2:9(ESV)

Through the Eyes of Grace

I've learned that my imperfections do not matter to Him because He said if any man/woman be "in Christ" we are made new. I now know that I am saved by grace, not by performance. Ephesians 2:8 says... God saved us through faith as an act of kindness. We had nothing to do with it. Being saved is a gift from God, GRACE! Grace is defined as ......

The freely given, unmerited favor and love of God; The influence or spirit of God operating in humans to regenerate or strengthen them.

Grace is a gift given by the Almighty God to His children... His royal children. As believers, **grace** and **royalty** is a part of our inheritance. However, they both come with responsibility.

Grace is more than unmerited favor. It is more than the material blessings we receive that we don't deserve. It is not a permission slip to justify selfish desires and not live up to our full potential. God's grace saves, then it enlightens. It saves, and then it uplifts.... It saves, and then it empowers and strengthens. Grace not only teaches us to do the right thing but infused grace empowers us to get the job done! Grace gives us that ability to walk according to His Word and know that we are who we are, only because of Him. Our royal position comes only through Him. We are daughters of the King. Being a daughter of the King has nothing to do with age, ethnicity, or family background.... It is all about God's GRACE.

Once we discover that nothing can separate us from God's love, we can then live free from the burden of living a life based on performance.

Romans 8, authored by Paul, the Apostle, depict God's inseparable love.

Nothing Can Separate Us from God's Love

[31]What then shall we say about these things? If God is for us, who can be against us? [32]He who didn't spare his own Son, but delivered him up for us all, how would he not also with him freely give us all things? [33]Who could bring a charge against God's chosen ones? It is God who justifies. [34]Who is he who condemns? It is Christ who died, yes rather, who was raised from the dead, who is at the right hand of God, who also makes intercession for us. [35]Who shall separate us from the love of Christ? Could oppression, or anguish, or persecution, or famine, or nakedness, or peril, or sword? [36]Even as it is written, "For your sake we are killed all day long. We were accounted as sheep for the slaughter." [37]No, in all these things, we are more than conquerors through him who loved us. [38]For I am persuaded, that

neither death, nor life, nor angels, nor principalities, nor things present, nor things to come, nor powers, [39]nor height, nor depth, nor any other created thing, will be able to

separate us from the love of God, which is in Christ Jesus our Lord.

ROMANS 8:31-39 (WEB)

"GRACE IS"

By Renee Johnson

Amazing grace so sweet it sounds
Grace saved someone like me...
I once was lost, but now I'm found,
Grace opened my eyes to see...

How long did I live accepting less than God
gives; Living life passive;
Looking for love in all the wrong places...

How long did it last, repeating my past;
Feeling like an outcast;
Trying to fit in all the wrong spaces...

Could it have been that deep within,
fear of rejection, led me to conform to
everything this world embraces?...

Was I more inclined to allow man-kind,
to control or define me, by gender

or what my race is?... Oh, but a

change came in time, that

transform my mind,

and led me to find

true peace;

Peace unshaken by different opinions or expressions of faces....

So, I no longer bow

To the scowl of one's brow;

My focus right now,

Is on how sweet and amazing God's **GRACE IS**!!!

But He has said to me, "My grace is sufficient for you [My loving-kindness and My mercy are more than enough—always available— regardless of the situation]; for [My] power is being perfected [and is completed and shows itself most effectively] in [your] weakness." Therefore, I will all the more gladly boast in my weaknesses, so that the power of Christ [may completely enfold me and] may dwell in me.

2 Corinthians 12:9 (AMP)

His grace brings eye opening revelations... Remember the hymn Amazing Grace... Once lost but now found.... Once blind but now seeing...It is grace that shined His light on us when we were in darkness. Grace empowers us to see light and to be light. It is where we find our strength and where we find our victorious identity. Grace looks beyond our faults and sees our needs. Grace changes our thought process. It allows us to think with the mind of Christ and not the mind of our soul (which is our mind, will, and emotions). It was the soul-ish part of Esau that caused him to forfeit his birthright. Your inheritance is worth more than your weary feelings. It is worth more than food for the physical body. It is your eternal blessing.

And let us not get tired of doing what is right, for after a while we will reap a harvest of blessing if we don't get discouraged and give up.

Galatians 6:9 (TLB)

What is your definition of grace?

_____

_____

_____

_____

_____

Can you relate to any section of the poem?

_____

_____

_____

_____

_____

Which section and why?

_____

_____

_____

_____

_____

Do you believe you have settled for less due to your view of yourself?

_____

_____

_____

_____

CHAPTER 8

RISE UP

FROM OBSCURITY TO NOTORIETY

¹Now Peter and John were going up to the temple at the hour of prayer, the ninth hour. ²And a man lame from birth was being carried, whom they laid daily at the gate of the temple that is called the Beautiful Gate to ask alms of those entering the temple. ³Seeing Peter and John about to go into the temple, he asked to receive alms. ⁴And Peter directed his gaze at him, as did John, and said, "Look at us." ⁵And he fixed his attention on them, expecting to receive something from them.

⁶But Peter said, "I have no silver and gold, but what I do have I give to you. In the name of Jesus Christ of Nazareth, rise up and walk!"

Acts 3:1-6 (ESV)

Chapter 8... 8 is the number of new beginnings.

Acts 3 is the perfect story of new beginnings.

This chapter is full of revelation so I'll start with two things for now. My first observation begins with noting the physical and mental posture of the lame man. Apparently, this man had no idea that healing was available to him. The lame man did not have the revelation knowledge, of the power, and authority, available to him through the Holy Spirit. Secondly, I want to bring your attention to Peter. Peter stood confident in the authority given to him through the Powerful Name of Jesus.

Peter and John walked in their royal position as "Authorized Carriers" of the Spirit of the living God. They believed that they were who God said they were and that they could do what God said they could do. "**Lord, help us to rise up and be who you created us to be and do what you created us to do.**"

Now, let's talk about the lame man. This man lying at the gate called Beautiful was not identified by his name; he was identified by his position (lying lame) and the amount of time he had been in that position (since birth). **Note- "We should never allow our position or condition to be the source of our identity."** The man was not lame due to the lack of God's power or God's desire to heal him. It was due to the lame man's lack of knowledge...The bible says, "We perish for the lack of knowledge". He had no knowledge that healing was available to him and that all he had to do was ask for it.

The scripture said that he asked for money... charitable gifts. He had faith for material things but he lacked faith in knowing that he could rise up and walk. I have heard people pray, asking God to pay their bills but refuse to pray for healing. Wow... We perish for the lack of knowledge. The lame man saw himself "lame", so he stayed in that position until someone came along, walking in their royal position, and offered him a new beginning. Up until that point, the lame man saw himself as just that... A lame man! I believe that as Peter stood in faith, spoke with confidence and authority, the lame man's faith was awakened. The power that brought the lame man to his feet was more than the touch of Peter's hand, it was his faith, by the power of the HOLY SPIRIT. Peter's faith was connected to the power and the authority given to him through the **NAME of JESUS**. Philippians 2:10-11 says "at the name of Jesus, every knee shall bow and every tongue shall confess that Jesus is Lord". No-thing is able to stand against the NAME of JESUS... There is power, in that Name ....

Peter had contagious faith in that NAME and the lame man caught it. Can you imagine what it was like for people to see this lame man walking after he had lain at the gate most of his life. The scripture says that the lame man went into the temple walking and leaping and praising God. The people in the temple recognized him as the man who sat begging for coins at the Beautiful Gate of the temple. They were filled with wonder and amazement *and* were mystified at what had happened to him. When we rise up and take our Royal place, our lives will become a testament of God's goodness. My Pastor (Caleb Moran) would say it like this..."God wants to use us as advertisement". The lame man emerged from obscurity to notoriety because of Peter and John walking in their God-given authority. Somebody is waiting for you at the gate... **Rise-up**...

My Uphill Journey

Along my 50-year journey, I have gone through swift transitions and the healthiness of my relationship with God has been a determining factor on how well I managed them.

For example, going from being a single parent (with 1 child) to marriage (adding 3 children) was definitely a transition. By the time we added the fifth child, the transition wasn't as bad as I had learned how to depend more on God. Later in my life (our life), I experienced another major transition. This transition was when my husband retired from the military. The move from being a U.S. Army Ranger and Green Beret, to the life of a civilian, was extremely challenging for him. It was also challenging for me. Although the previous transitions were difficult, the most challenging for the both of us was the passing of my parents (2 years apart on the same date...May 8th), and having an empty nest... (all within a 4-year period of time). For the last 4 years, I was helping my sisters care for our parents as their health was deteriorating, and for the last 25 years, I was mommy from sun up to sundown... Suddenly, one day, both of my parents were gone to be with the Lord, and the last of our kids had left the nest... We had officially become "empty nesters". Wow...what did this mean? Was my identity built upon being a daughter, a mother, or a military wife? I must admit, for a moment there, I was slightly shaken. I had to regroup and grab a hold tomy anchor. My true anchor was not in a title, or my responsibilities. My anchor is in Christ Jesus. Being anchored in Christ Jesus led me to the Word of God. That is where I would find the promise that applied to my circumstances. I had to come into the knowledge of the truth of God's Word. I had to "rise up". Ephesians 2:10 says... "God has made us what we are, and in our union with Christ Jesus he has created us for a life of good deeds, which he has already prepared for us to do." In order to know what he has prepared for us to do, we must ask Him...The bible says, [7]"Ask, and it will be given to you; seek, and you will find; knock, and it will be opened to you. For everyone who asks receives, and he who seeks finds, and to him who knocks it will be open (Matthew 7:7-8) .... Seek Him for direction. Hebrews 11:6 says "He is a rewarder of those who diligently seek Him." In my seeking, God revealed that my "good deeds" in being a caregiver for my parents and having my nest filled with children had come to an end. It was time to transition to the next season. As one season ends, another begins. We must move into the new and be willing to let go of the old. We must "rise-up"!!!

You will show me the path of life. In your presence is fullness of joy. In your right hand there are pleasures forever more.

Psalm 16:11 (WEB)

Time to Rise

It has been through my developing a relationship with God that I started to see myself the way God sees me. Developing a relationship with God is a constant process. Let us not forfeit our inheritance due to lack of seeking Him and believing that He is who He says He is, and He will do what He says He will do. We must also believe that we are who He says we are and we can do what He says we can do. We must Rise-up!!!

'Call to Me and I will answer you, and tell you [and even show you] great and mighty things, [things which have been confined and hidden], which you do not know *and* understand *and* cannot distinguish.'
Jeremiah 33:3 (AMP)

We must not allow situations or circumstances surrounding us to affect our relationship with the Father. The bible says..." many are the afflictions of the righteous, But the Lord delivers him out of them all" (Psalms 34:19). We must not allow our afflictions to hold us bondage and blind us from the opportunities and possibilities that have been laid before us. Keeping our eyes on the promise, and keeping first things first, truly makes the difference. Matthew 6:33 says...

"But more than anything else put God's work first and do what he wants" ... then the other things will be yours as well. Keeping things in order strengthens the relationship. Additionally, strengthening any relationship, in the physical, and in the spiritual, requires **communication.** The lines of communication should always be open. It is a 2-way process...a process of talking and listening... Not only should we be talking to God, we should also be listening to God. Looking in retrospect, the times when I talked more than I listened, I found myself getting off track... When you are off track, you're not ready for the next turn/transition. It is this relationship with the Father, through the Son, that gives us our

"true identity". It's the power of the Holy Spirit that empowers us to stay on track and take our royal position.

Romans 8:11 says that the same power that raised Jesus from the dead, is alive in us as believers. That resurrecting spirit says that we are victorious, we are strong, we are triumphant, we are more than conquerors, and greater is **HE** that lives within us than He that is in the world. We are above and not beneath, we are blessed in the city and in the field, we are crowned with glory and honor. We are a royal priesthood, and we have authority as children of the King. It is now time to use that authority.

"Rise-Up" ... You areRoyalty!

My Prayer for You...

I pray that you will begin to walk in the true destiny that Father God has created for you. Refuse to allow yourself to get lost in life's transitions. Stand firm on the Word of God and the promises of God... He and His Word is the same yesterday, today, and forever more. Remember, when storms arise and road blocks are before you, reading your manufacturer's manual (THE HOLY BILBLE) is imperative. The Manual will always lead you to a place of refuge.

I hope that you have been enlightened, encouraged, revived, and renewed by every word that you have read. Stay hungry and thirsty for the Word of God.

He shall satisfy the hungry soul with good things. ... **Believe** to see God's Word and His promises manifested in your life. David said he would have given up unless he believed to see the goodness of the Lord in the land of the living. So, I encourage you to commit to following these 3 steps:

1) **Believe** God is who He says He is...

2) **Believe** you are who God says you are...

3) Every day, **LIVE LIKE YOU BELIEVE!!!**

If there is anyone reading this book and you have not accepted Jesus Christ as your Lord and Savior, it is not too late. Say the following prayer, confessing with your mouth and believing in your heart...

Heavenly Father,

I confess and repent of my sins; I ask you now to create in me a clean heart and renew a right sprit within me. I confess with my mouth, and believe in my heart, that you sent your Son Jesus, to die for me, rise up for me, and give me everlasting victory. I accept Jesus Christ as my Lord and Savior and I know that my life is forever changed. **In Jesus' Name...**

Your New Life Has Begun!!!!!

DAILY AFFIRMATIONS

- **I see myself as God sees me; I was created in His likeness.**

- **I am the temple of the Holy Spirit.**

- **I practice the things that are pleasing to God, walking by faith and not by sight.**

- **I do not walk in the spirit of timidity; I walk in the spirit of LOVE, power, and a sound mind.**

- **I am fearfully and wonderfully made by God; created to give him glory.**

- **My Father has a plan for my life; a plan of hope and prosperity.**

- **God's love for me is unfailing for I am the apple of his eye.**

- **I walk according to Kingdom principles stirring up goodness, peace and joy from the Holy Spirit.**

- **Integrity and uprightness preserve me.**

- **My thoughts consist of things that are true, honest, just, pure, lovely, and of good report.**

- **I complete assignments with an attitude of excellence (at home, at school and on my job) as unto the Lord.**

- **I am more than a conqueror and I can do all things through Christ who strengthens me.**

- **The Lord is on my side; I will not fear.**

JOURNAL

REFERENCES

-Note: The translations used for most scriptures are as marked, KJV used otherwise. (The Holy Bible... AMP, CEV, ESV, GNT, GW, MSG, NIV, NLT, TLB, WEB)

-Maximizing Your Potential....... Myles Munroe

-Abba's Child: The Cry of the Heart for   Intimate Belonging ......Brennan Manning

-Your Move/The Blame Game (http://subsplash.com/yourmove/v/e7cc65b) Andy Stanley

-Hold to God's Unchanging Hand (Hymn) Jennie B. Wilson

-The Spirit of Faith ......Mark Hankins

-National Institute of Mental Health (https://www.nimh.nih.gov/)

-Post-Traumatic Growth Research Group – UNC Charlotte (https://ptgiuncc.edu/) Dept. of Psychology

-Word Reference Dictionary (http://www.wordreference.com/definition/Grace)

ABOUT THE AUTHOR

Renee is a loving wife, mother, grandmother, sister, and friend. She is more than an author. Renee is an Ordained Minister, and a Spoken-Word Artist (aka J. Renee). She lives her life using her gifts and talents to glorify God and help build His Kingdom.

Her passion for life is shown in her caring for her family and giving back to her community. She believes that whom much is given, much is required.

Her parents, the late Pastor Willie & Orleana S. Minor, encouraged her to get an education, and to live a life being more of a contributor than a consumer.

She is a native of Rayville, La. and a graduate of the University of Louisiana-Monroe formerly known as Northeast Louisiana University.

Renee is the youngest of three girls. Her two sisters are currently educators in North Louisiana schools. (Amanda Gail Simmons in Lincoln Parish and Shelia Minor in Morehouse Parish).

Renee is the CEO of The ChampionsWithin Kingdom Builders and she is married to Terry "Ranger" Johnson, Sr. Terry and Renee currently reside in Lafayette, La.

Made in the USA
Columbia, SC
27 December 2017